THE SINKING OF THE
TITANIC

Craig E. Blohm

ReferencePoint
Press

San Diego, CA

About the Author

Craig E. Blohm has written numerous books and magazine articles for young readers. He and his wife, Desiree, reside in Tinley Park, Illinois.

© 2020 ReferencePoint Press, Inc.
Printed in the United States

For more information, contact:
ReferencePoint Press, Inc.
PO Box 27779
San Diego, CA 92198
www.ReferencePointPress.com

LIBRARY OF CONGRESS CATALOGING-IN-PUBLICATION DATA

Name: Blohm, Craig E., 1948– author.
Title: The Sinking of the *Titanic*/by Craig E. Blohm.
Description: San Diego, CA: ReferencePoint Press, Inc., 2020. | Series:
   Historic Disasters and Mysteries | Includes bibliographical references and index.
Identifiers: LCCN 2018051670 (print) | LCCN 2018053340 (ebook) | ISBN
   9781682826362 (eBook) | ISBN 9781682826355 (hardback)
Subjects: LCSH: *Titanic* (Steamship)—Juvenile literature. | Shipwrecks—North
   Atlantic Ocean—History—20th century—Juvenile literature. |
   Disasters—North Atlantic Ocean—History—20th century—Juvenile literature.
Classification: LCC G530.T6 (ebook) | LCC G530.T6 B596 2020 (print) | DDC
   910.9163/4—dc23
LC record available at https://lccn.loc.gov/2018051670

CONTENTS

An Ill-Fated Voyage

The RMS *Titanic* was the most magnificent ship to ever set sail—larger, more elegant, and believed to be safer than any other vessel afloat. Amid fanfare and ceremony, the *Titanic* left Southampton, England, for its maiden voyage on April 10, 1912. After picking up passengers at Cherbourg, France, and Queenstown, Ireland, the mighty vessel headed out to sea. On board were 2,223 passengers and crew traveling across the Atlantic Ocean to New York City. Most of them would never reach their destination. On April 14 the *Titanic* struck an iceberg in the North Atlantic some 1,300 miles (2,092 km) from New York. In less than three hours, the ship that many called unsinkable plunged to the bottom of the ocean, taking with it the lives of more than 1,500 people.

The sinking of the *Titanic*, one of the greatest maritime tragedies in history, still fascinates millions of people. There are heroic accounts of men remaining behind as their wives and children were rowed to safety in lifeboats and of stokers who kept the *Titanic*'s boilers running even as water flooded the bottom of the ship. But there are also stories of cowardice, of men who jumped into lifeboats ahead of the women and children designated to go first and of a man who tried to steal the life jacket off a wireless radio operator who was desperately sending distress signals.

A Human Tragedy

The story of the *Titanic* disaster is also a cautionary tale of hubris, a word seldom heard today. It means an excess of pride, an arrogance that can often lead to disaster. The builders of the *Titanic* were confident that their new ship would be the safest vessel afloat, an attitude that allowed them to overlook design flaws in their ship. It led to so-called watertight compartments that were, in fact, not completely watertight, and a complement of lifeboats that fell well short of the number of people on board. During an April 21 memorial service for *Titanic* victims, Bishop Edward Talbot proclaimed, "*Titanic,* name and thing, will stand as a monument and warning to human presumption."[1]

A common misconception is that the *Titanic* was publicized as unsinkable. The White Star Line, the owner of the *Titanic*, never claimed its new ship could *not* sink, only that it was *designed* to be unsinkable. But by the time the *Titanic* sailed, the public had gained the impression of a ship that was indestructible. Several passengers later recalled hearing an exchange between passenger Sylvia Caldwell and a deckhand as Caldwell boarded the *Titanic* for its maiden voyage. She is said to have asked whether the ship was safe. The deckhand replied, "God Himself could not sink this ship."[2]

A Matter of Class

If the *Titanic* was an example of hubris, it was also a reflection of the Edwardian period in Great Britain, a time of peace and prosperity named for King Edward VII. It was an era of inflexible rules of conduct in a society marked by the strict separation of the classes. Socializing between the rich upper class and the domestic lower class was unthinkable. Servants lived and worked in the basement rooms of opulent mansions, catering to the needs of the rich who occupied the floors above. The *Titanic* echoed this class system in both location and amenities. The wealthiest passengers traveled in first class, occupying luxurious accom-

A hand-colored glass slide from 1912 captures the historic maiden (and only) voyage of the Titanic steaming out of its home port of Southhampton.

modations on the upper decks of the ship. Second-class passengers traveled in similar, if not quite as lavish, spaces. Third class, comprising mostly of poor immigrants, inhabited the lower decks, a space often referred to as steerage for its location near the engines and steering machinery.

Crowded into noisy and hot third-class cabins and dormitories, immigrants were prohibited from entering first- or second-class areas. Once the *Titanic* struck the iceberg, first- and second-class passengers had ready access to the lifeboats. Third-class passengers, however, had to navigate a maze of confusing passageways from deep within the ship while following instructions given by the crew in English, which was a language many of them could not understand. It is not surprising then that 62 percent of first-class passengers survived but only 25 percent of third-class passengers did so.

The End of an Era

The sinking of the *Titanic* is sometimes seen as a sign of the decline of the Edwardian age. Two years later, the era's peace and prosperity was shattered by the onset of World War I. But before the carnage of war engulfed Europe, mighty ships like the *Titanic* catered to the extravagances of the rich while offering the poor a chance to begin a new life in America. The story of the *Titanic* is timeless, rich in drama and tragedy, full of noble bravery and disgraceful cowardice. More than one hundred years later, it still fascinates the world.

CHAPTER ONE

The Magnificent
Titanic

On a warm evening in the summer of 1907, a small but elegant dinner party at the stately Downshire House in London, England, was nearing its end. The mansion's residents, Lord William James Pirrie and his wife, Lady Margaret, and their guests, J. Bruce and Florence Ismay, had enjoyed a pleasant evening of fine food and polite conversation. But now the talk between the two men turned to a more serious subject: the state of transatlantic shipping.

The transportation of cargo and passengers between Europe and the United States was one of the major industries of the era. By the early twentieth century, the age of sail had given way to steel steamships that could cross the Atlantic Ocean in days instead of weeks. Great Britain, the United States, France, Germany, and other countries fiercely competed for the lucrative transatlantic routes. Ismay and Pirrie each had a strong connection to the sea and an interest in developing its business potential. Ismay was the chairman and managing director of the White Star Line, a prominent British shipping company. Pirrie was the chairman of the world's largest shipbuilder, Harland and Wolff, in Belfast, Ireland.

White Star Line's main competitor was the Cunard Steamship Company, a British line noted for its fast passenger ships. Cunard was poised to triumph in its rivalry against White Star with two new ocean liners, the RMS *Lusitania* and the RMS *Mauretania*, which were scheduled to enter the Atlantic service by late 1907. Ismay knew his own company had to build new ships to compete with Cunard or risk bankruptcy. Pirrie, too, was caught up in the battle between White Star and Cunard. Harland and Wolff owned the rights to be the exclusive construction and repair facility for all future White Star vessels. If White Star foundered, Harland and Wolff could suffer a disastrous loss.

By the end of the evening, Ismay and Pirrie had agreed to build three ocean liners to rival Cunard's new vessels. These ships would be longer, wider, and heavier than any previous liner. Instead of trying to beat Cunard's *Lusitania* and *Mauretania* in transatlantic speed, Ismay's ships would be designed to give passengers the safest and most luxurious voyage imaginable. The new liners would be given names befitting the two men's grand vision: *Olympic*, *Titanic*, and *Gigantic*.

Pirrie drew sketches depicting his ideas of how the grand new ocean liners would look. The next step was to turn those sketches into detailed plans.

Designing the *Titanic*

Nearly every workday since he was fifteen years old, Thomas Andrews had entered the Harland and Wolff shipyard and settled down to work. An energetic and industrious young man, Andrews had always been interested in ships and the sea. "Quite early," author Shan F. Bullock wrote in 1912, "young Tom, like many another lad, developed a fondness for boats, and because of his manifest skill in the making of these he gained among his friends the nickname of 'Admiral.'"[3] In addition, Andrews was Lord Pirrie's nephew. Beginning his career in 1889 as an apprentice at Harland and Wolff, Andrews learned every aspect of shipbuilding, from riveting and engine building to painting and cabinetry. He also learned ship design, and by 1901 Andrews had risen to the position of director of the Harland and Wolff design department. In 1907 he became the managing director of the shipyard.

In the fall of that year, a design team of Andrews, Alexander Carlisle, and Edward Wilding began drafting the plans for the three new White Star liners. The first two ships were assigned hull numbers 400 and 401 (they would later receive their names, *Olympic* and *Titanic*) and were scheduled to be built side by side. The construction of the third would not begin until after 400 and 401 were completed.

Working under huge skylights in the Harland and Wolff drafting room, the designers drew detailed plans for a ship 882 feet, 9 inches (269 m) long and 92 feet, 6 inches (28 m) wide. Twenty-nine coal-fired boilers provided steam for two powerful reciprocat-

A photograph taken between 1910 and 1911 at the Harland and Wolff dock in Belfast, Ireland, shows the Titanic's three huge propellers.

ing steam engines and one rotary steam turbine that turned the three huge propellers to drive the *Titanic* across the Atlantic. Since the Cunard ships had four funnels, or smokestacks, the designers decided that the *Titanic* would have four also, to provide the appearance of a ship powerful enough to rival the *Lusitania* and the *Mauretania*. The *Titanic* had two masts that supported the antenna for the ship's wireless radio system. Attached to the forward mast was the crow's nest, where lookouts would scan the horizon for any signs of danger ahead.

The *Titanic*'s Safety Features

Lord Pirrie wanted his ships not only to be beautiful but safe as well. Fifteen lateral bulkheads, or walls, extended above the ship's waterline and divided the lower decks of the *Titanic* into sixteen watertight compartments. In an emergency, watertight doors in twelve of these bulkheads could be quickly shut to prevent water from flowing into adjoining compartments. The *Titanic* could remain afloat with any two compartments, or the first four compartments, flooded.

The ship would carry sixteen wooden lifeboats, numbered 1 through 16, and four wood-and-canvas collapsible boats, identified as A through D, with a total capacity of 1,178 people. This was more than the Board of Trade, the body responsible for all British maritime activities, required ocean liners to have. Many maritime experts, including Carlisle, considered these regulations outdated in light of the new, larger vessels being built by White Star and Cunard. But the prevailing wisdom was that, if a ship became disabled, the lifeboats could ferry passengers to a rescue vessel and then return to pick up more. By design, the *Titanic*'s boat deck could accommodate up to sixty-four lifeboats. But White Star kept the number at twenty, so as not to clutter the deck where passengers would be strolling.

On July 28, 1908, Ismay approved the plans for the *Titanic*. It was time to build the largest moving object ever designed by human hands.

Constructing the *Titanic*

Construction of the *Titanic's* hull began on March 31, 1909, when the keel was laid. Soon a framework of iron ribs began to take shape, creating the skeleton of the new ship. After the skeleton was complete, workers used rivets to attach giant steel plates to the skeleton to form the hull and the bulkheads that divided the ship into its watertight compartments. The rivets, bolt-like fasteners made of iron or steel, were heated until they were red-hot and were then hammered into place either mechanically or by skilled workers. The *Titanic* was held together by 3 million rivets weighing a total of 1,200 tons (1,089 t).

It took some three thousand laborers working day and night shifts to build the huge vessel. On May 31, 1911, the ship, minus its funnels, interior furnishings, and machinery, was ready to be launched. In a festive ceremony, grandstands were filled with thousands of people, including Andrews, Ismay, and Lord Pirrie, who were eager to see their creation enter the water. At 12:13 p.m. the *Titanic* slid down the slipway, accompanied by a cacophony of tugboat whistles, foghorns, and cheers from the crowd. In just over a minute, the massive black hull of ship number 401, now officially the *Titanic*, floated serenely in the waters of Belfast Lough, an inlet from the Irish Sea.

Fitting Out and Sea Trials

Over the next ten months, the *Titanic* was fitted with its boilers, engines, propellers, funnels, and other mechanical parts of the ship. Once these were in place, skilled artisans went to work creating the interior of the ship. No expense was spared in making the *Titanic* as luxurious as the finest European hotel. "The aim," says author and historian Anton Gill, "was to make the facilities even more alluring to the wealthy, especially Americans, who were prepared to

When the *Titanic* set sail on April 10, 1912, some of the richest people in the world were aboard. The wealthiest passenger was John Jacob Astor IV, an American businessman who had made his fortune in real estate, including building what is today New York's Waldorf Astoria hotel. Astor stayed behind after putting his wife into a lifeboat, and he perished in the sinking. At the time of his death, he was worth $87 million, about $2.26 billion in today's dollars.

Benjamin Guggenheim, another prominent businessman, slept through the collision with the iceberg. Upon being awakened, he dressed in formal evening clothes and headed to the deck with his personal assistant, commenting, "We've dressed up in our best and are prepared to go down like gentlemen." Guggenheim's body was never recovered.

Isidor Straus was the wealthy co-owner of New York's famous Macy's department store. He and his wife, Ida, were returning from a winter in Europe aboard the *Titanic*. Refusing to enter a lifeboat without her husband, Ida and Isidor remained on deck as the *Titanic* sank, perishing together after a life of forty years together.

One millionaire who was expected to sail on the *Titanic* but did not was John Pierpont (J.P.) Morgan. As head of the International Mercantile Marine Company, the owner of the White Star Line, Morgan had his own luxurious suite aboard the *Titanic*. But at the last minute he canceled his reservation, a move that undoubtedly saved his life.

Quoted in *Encyclopedia Titanica*, "Mr Benjamin Guggenheim." www.encyclopedia-titanica.org.

pay very large sums to cross the Atlantic in style."[4] Elegance could be found everywhere; the furnishings in the first-class staterooms and dining saloons included ornate crystal chandeliers, richly embroidered carpeting, and fine china place settings.

The most remarkable example of the *Titanic*'s extravagant style was the Grand Staircase. This sweeping stairway, situated under a wrought iron and glass dome, was 20 feet (6 m) wide by 57 feet (17 m) high and was paneled in English oak. Designed exclusively for first-class passengers, the staircase allowed them to elegantly descend from their cabins on the highest deck to public rooms on the decks below.

On April 2, 1912, the *Titanic* was ready to begin sea trials to make sure everything was ready for its maiden voyage. At 6:00 a.m. it put out to sea, running tests of speed, maneuverability, turning, and stopping. The ship's equipment, from engines and boilers to compasses and electrical systems, was thoroughly tested. After the day of sea trials was over, the *Titanic* had passed with flying colors and was pronounced ready to sail by a representative of the Board of Trade. At 8:00 p.m. the *Titanic* left Belfast to pick up passengers at Southampton, England, and Cherbourg, France. It then steamed to Queenstown (now Cobh), Ireland, to pick up the last passengers for its maiden voyage to New York City.

The Route of the *Titanic*

The voyage of the RMS *Titanic* began in Belfast, Ireland. The ship sailed to Southampton, England; Cherbourg, France; and Queenstown, Ireland, to pick up passengers. The ship sank before reaching its final destination of New York City.

Life at Sea

At 1:30 p.m. on Thursday, April 11, the *Titanic* set sail from Queenstown with 2,223 passengers and crew aboard. The ship was under the firm hand of her captain, sixty-two-year-old Edward J. Smith, an experienced seaman who had been commanding White Star ships since 1895. Among those aboard were the two men who certainly had the most interest in seeing how the *Titanic* fared on its maiden voyage: designer Andrews and owner Ismay.

For the 329 first-class passengers, the *Titanic* was as luxurious as the finest London hotels. "What a ship!" wrote Ida Straus, the wife of wealthy American businessman Isidor Straus. "Our rooms are furnished in the best of taste and most luxuriously. . . . They are really rooms, not cabins."[5] There was plenty for the first-class passengers to do on the *Titanic*. Strolling along the decks, relaxing in a deck chair, browsing the library, or listening to the ship's eight-piece orchestra were all popular pastimes. There were smoking rooms for men and writing rooms for women. For those interested in more physical activities, the gymnasium was filled with weights, stationary bicycles, and mechanical horses for riding. After exercising, a swim in the heated pool or a session in the Turkish bath steam room refreshed a tired body. For second-class passengers, shuffleboard, chess, and other games provided active fun. Although few activities were organized for them, the third-class passengers gathered on the deck at the ship's stern to relax and play games.

First-class meals on the *Titanic* were elegantly served in several dining rooms. Passengers dressed in their finest tuxedos and evening gowns to feast on eleven-course meals in the dining saloon, a room that could accommodate more than five hundred diners. The 285 second-class passengers had their own dining

> **Did You Know?**
> To feed its passengers, the *Titanic* carried 75,000 pounds of meat, 40 tons of potatoes, 1,500 gallons of milk, and 11,000 pounds of fresh fish—among other items.

The *Titanic* carried more than passengers on its maiden voyage. Deep in the ship on the lower decks, the *Titanic's* cargo holds carried an astonishing assortment of goods bound for the United States. The following items were among the cargo:

12 cases of ostrich feathers
1,514 bags of potatoes
586 cases of cheese
2 barrels of mercury
412 cases of walnuts
76 cases of "dragon's blood" (a tree resin used in folk medicine)
3 cases of tennis balls
1 box of golf balls
1 case of motion-picture film
15 cases of peas
1 case of rabbit fur
2 grandfather clocks

Also on board were a brand-new 1912 Renault Type CB Coupe de Ville automobile and a jeweled edition of *The Rubaiyat of Omar Khayyam*, a book of Persian poetry. Adorned with more than one thousand rubies, garnets, amethysts, and topazes, the *Rubaiyat* sold for about $2,000 just months before the voyage. Today, its value—if undamaged—would be at least $40,000. In all, the *Titanic's* cargo was worth $420,000—almost $11 million in today's dollars.

facilities, which, although less elegant than in first class, were equal to the best accommodations on other lines' ships. Three-course meals were served to the accompaniment of piano music. In third class, the 710 passengers ate in two rather plain dining rooms, seated at long tables. They were served simple but hearty fare such as roast beef, boiled potatoes, and fruit.

The Calm Before the Disaster

The *Titanic's* passengers settled into a comfortable routine as the voyage continued, including strolling the decks, exercising in the gymnasium, sending messages called Marconigrams (named for

Guglielmo Marconi, the inventor of wireless radio), and placing friendly wagers on how many miles the ship had traveled that day. In those first days, all was as it should be. Andrews was on board to investigate any problems with the ship. After inspecting the *Titanic* from stem to stern, he found only minor concerns, such as the color of a deck being too dark or having too many screws on the passenger coat hooks.

The sea was so calm that many passengers felt they were not on a ship at all. "At all times," wrote San Francisco doctor Washington Dodge, "one might walk the decks, with the same security as if walking down [San Francisco's] Market Street, so little motion there was to the vessel."[6] Not all passengers shared Dodge's confidence in the ship. Thirty-two-year-old fashion journalist Edith Rosenbaum was returning home on the *Titanic* from a business trip to Paris. In a letter she wrote to her secretary before sailing, Rosenbaum remarked, "Am going to take my very much needed rest on this trip, but I cannot get over my feeling of depression and premonition of trouble. How I wish it were over!"[7]

As night enveloped the *Titanic* on Sunday, April 14, 1912, Rosenbaum's wish was about to be realized. But it would not happen in the way she expected.

CHAPTER TWO

Disaster Strikes

It was a moonless night with millions of stars blazing overhead as the *Titanic*, four-and-a-half days out of Southhampton, sliced through the frigid waters of the North Atlantic some 1,300 miles (2,092 km) from its destination, New York City. The nearest land was Cape Race, Newfoundland, about 350 miles (563 km) north. The *Titanic*'s engines were driving the ship at 22.5 knots, or 26 miles per hour (42 kmh), just under its top speed. In the crow's nest, lookouts Frederick Fleet and Reginald Lee scanned the dark for signs of danger.

In the North Atlantic, the main hazard at this time of year was icebergs. Most of these icebergs came from the western coast of Greenland, floating south into the Atlantic shipping lanes. Ships traveling this route usually reduced their speed, stopping if safe passage became impossible. On the night of April 14, however, the *Titanic* did not slow down.

Warnings Ignored

In the *Titanic*'s wireless room, senior operator Jack Phillips was busy receiving messages from other ships while struggling to transmit a backlog of Marconigrams from the *Titanic*'s passengers. These messages were sent by Morse code, which consisted of a series of dots and dashes representing letters and numbers. Passengers paid a small sum to send greetings to friends and relatives.

At 9:40 p.m. a message came in from the SS *Mesaba* that read, in part, "Saw much heavy pack ice and great number of large icebergs, also field ice."[8] Such a message would ordinarily be given to an officer on the bridge, the *Titanic*'s control center. But Phillips was overwhelmed by the passenger communications that still had to be transmitted, so he placed the message under a paperweight on his desk. At 11:05 p.m. another ship, the SS *Californian,* transmitted, "Say, Old Man, we are stopped and surrounded by ice." This message also never reached the bridge. Instead, an exasperated Phillips sent an angry reply: "Shut up. Shut up. I am busy. I am working Cape Race."[9]

Collision

Lookouts Fleet and Lee tried to keep alert despite the bitter temperature, which had plummeted to 32°F (0°C). Their task was made more difficult by the moonless night and glassy sea, making it hard to discern objects in the ship's path.

At 11:39 p.m. Fleet saw a dark mass in the water perhaps 500 yards (457 m) ahead. He immediately reached up and rang the emergency bell three times, the signal for an object in the ship's path. Then he picked up the crow's nest telephone and called the bridge, speaking three ominous words: "Iceberg right ahead."[10] Receiving this warning, the officer in charge on the bridge, First Officer William Murdoch, ordered the ship's helmsman, Quartermaster Robert Hichens, to turn the *Titanic* away from the iceberg. This, he hoped, would avert a head-on collision. Hichens began spinning the large steering wheel as fast as he could. At the same time, Murdoch signaled the engineering crew in the depths of the ship to stop the engines, and he threw the switch to close the ship's watertight doors.

Did You Know?
The iceberg that the *Titanic* struck was estimated to weigh some 83 million tons and had floated south after breaking away from a Greenland glacier around 1908.

For agonizing seconds, the ship steamed straight ahead. Then, slowly, the *Titanic* began turning. Its bow gradually swung to port, or left, presenting its starboard, or right, side to the looming tower

A wireless operator on board an ocean liner transcribes a message. This job, depicted in a hand-colored slide from 1912, would also have been done on the Titanic *before it reached its tragic end.*

of ice. Just when it seemed that the ship would clear the iceberg, a slight shudder, accompanied by a scraping sound, indicated that the *Titanic* had collided with the underwater part of the iceberg. The date was April 14; the time was 11:40 p.m.

Captain Smith, who was in the ship's chart room at the time of the collision, rushed to the bridge and asked Murdoch what the ship had struck. "An iceberg, Sir," Murdoch replied. "I hard-a-starboarded and reversed the engines. I was going to hard-a-port around it, but she was too close."[11] Smith, along with Andrews, who had just arrived on the bridge, began an inspection tour belowdecks. It was not long before the *Titanic's* situation became clear. Icy water was flooding into several of the watertight compartments through breaches in the hull. After their inspection, Smith and Andrews were joined by Ismay in the captain's cabin. Andrews had calculated the outcome of the damage, and now he delivered the grim news. With six compartments taking on water, there was no way the ship could survive. Andrews estimated that the *Titanic* had only an hour to an hour and a half before it would sink.

Women and Children First

While Smith was receiving the news of the *Titanic*'s fate, most of the passengers were unaware that anything had happened. Many felt only a slight jar or vibration as the ship hit the iceberg, certainly nothing that would cause alarm. As first-class passenger Ella White later described the moment, "It was just as though we went over about a thousand marbles. There was nothing terrifying about it at all."[12]

At 12:05 a.m. on April 15, twenty-five minutes after the collision, Smith ordered his deck officers to prepare the lifeboats for launching and inform the passengers to put on their life jackets and assemble on the boat deck. Then he went to the wireless room and told Phillips to begin sending "CQD," the maritime distress signal. Phillips tapped out, "Require immediate assistance. Come at once. We struck an iceberg. Sinking."[13] Through his headphones, Phillips soon heard the Cunard ship RMS *Carpathia* responding to his transmission: "Do you require assistance?" Phillips replied, "Yes. Come quick."[14]

The *Titanic*'s stewards were going from cabin to cabin, urging passengers to dress warmly and put on their life jackets. As passengers began arriving on the boat deck, there was confusion but no panic. "There was no excitement whatever," recalled White. "Nobody seemed frightened. Nobody was panic-stricken."[15] The orchestra assembled on deck and began playing a series of popular tunes to reassure the passengers.

Did You Know?
Some experts believe that if the *Titanic* had hit the iceberg head-on, it could have remained afloat until help arrived.

First Officer Murdoch and Second Officer Charles Lightoller were in charge of loading the lifeboats. By order of the captain, women and children were to board the lifeboats first. The process of filling the boats was problematic at best. Some passengers believed the trouble to be minor and preferred to wait on deck until the crisis was past rather than board a small, fragile lifeboat.

Many women refused to go without their husbands. At 12:45 a.m. the first lifeboat, number seven, with a capacity of sixty-five passengers, was lowered into the sea. Due to the reluctance of the female passengers, who had to be persuaded or forced to enter the lifeboat, only twenty-eight people were on board as it descended to the water below.

While the passengers were boarding the lifeboats, Phillips, now assisted by junior operator Harold Bride, continued to send out distress signals. Around the same time, a bright flash illuminated the darkness, streaking high into the sky and exploding with a loud boom and a shower of brilliant white stars. It was the first of eight or more rockets fired by the *Titanic* crew to signal a ship that had been spotted nearby. The ship was estimated to be between 5 and 10 miles (8 and 16 km) from the *Titanic*—close enough for it to come to the stricken liner's aid. But it had not responded to the *Titanic's* wireless distress calls and sat motionless in the water.

Two Ships

The ship was the *Californian*, whose wireless operator, Cyril Evans, had been rebuked by Phillips's angry message to "Shut up!" about an hour earlier. Evans had shut down his wireless station for the night and gone to bed. The *Californian's* second officer, Herbert Stone, came on duty at midnight. He was informed of a large ship off in the distance, the lights from her portholes and decks glowing. Not knowing it was the *Titanic*, Stone began signaling with a Morse lamp, a strong spotlight that could send Morse code visually. He asked the ship for its identity. He received no reply but soon observed a white rocket shooting skyward from the liner.

The *Californian's* captain, Stanley Lord, had retired after a long day of sailing, but Stone woke him and informed him that a ship in the distance had fired a rocket. Lord replied that it was probably just a company signal (launched by ships as identification to other vessels), and he returned to bed. After seeing several more rockets, however, Stone was still concerned. "A ship is not going to fire rockets at sea for nothing," he said to another officer on

The Fate of the Third-Class Passengers

While first-class passengers on the *Titanic* enjoyed all of the luxuries money could buy, third-class passengers had few comforts. Lack of comfort ultimately proved to be the least of the problems for those relegated to the lower decks of the ship. Three-quarters of the third-class passengers perished when the ship sank.

In the chaos of the moment, third-class passengers were almost forgotten as the other passengers were boarding lifeboats. Various obstacles made survival even less likely for those on the lower decks. Fewer stewards had been assigned to third class, and many of those spoke only English—making it difficult for foreigners to understand their instructions. In addition, access to the boat deck passed through a maze of long, narrow, confusing passages and stairways that even confused many of the stewards who worked on the lower decks. By the time many third-class passengers finally reached the boat deck, most of the lifeboats had left the ship.

Several books and movies have suggested that third-class passengers were deliberately locked in the lower decks to keep them from gaining access to the lifeboats. Fearing the spread of disease, US immigration regulations did require gates to keep third-class passengers from mingling with the rest of the passengers. It is possible that some of these gates remained locked, preventing some third-class passengers from reaching the boat deck. There is no evidence, however, to support the idea that this was anything more than an oversight during a time of extreme stress.

the *Californian*'s bridge. "There must be something wrong with her."[16] Stone again awakened Lord, but the captain simply acknowledged his concern and went back to sleep.

While the *Californian* lay silent in the water, 58 miles (93 km) southeast of the *Titanic*, Captain Arthur Rostron of the *Carpathia* had changed course and was steaming toward the stricken White Star liner. A single-funnel passenger ship, the *Carpathia* was smaller and slower than the *Titanic*, with a top speed of 14 knots, or 16 miles per hour (30 kmh). To make sure he got the most speed possible, Rostron ordered more crewmen to the boiler rooms and shut off the heat and hot water in the ship to direct maximum steam to the engines. Rostron estimated that it would take four hours to reach the *Titanic*'s position. As the bow of the

When *Titanic* lookout Frederick Fleet saw the iceberg some 500 yards (457 m) away in the ship's path, it left little time for Quartermaster Robert Hichens to maneuver the ship to avoid a collision. Since then, many have wondered if using binoculars might have helped prevent the disaster.

The White Star line issued binoculars for all of its ships, and the lookouts usually kept theirs in the crow's nest. Shortly after the *Titanic* set sail, however, the binoculars were nowhere to be found. A search turned up nothing, so the ship sailed on without the missing "lookout glasses," as they were known aboard ships of the time. But the binoculars *were* on board. Just before the *Titanic* left port, several officers were reassigned. First Officer Charles Lightoller became the ship's second officer, replacing David Blair, who remained behind in Southampton. Blair was in charge of the binoculars and had put them in a locker in his cabin, neglecting to tell anyone where they were. When he left the ship, he inadvertently took the key to the locker with him.

During the investigation into the sinking, Fleet testified that having binoculars would have helped him see the iceberg in time to avoid a collision. But captains of other ships felt that binoculars for lookouts were unnecessary because their job was to simply report an object, not identify it through close examination with binoculars.

Blair kept the key, eventually passing it on to his daughter. In 2007 it was sold at auction for about £90,000, or approximately $180,000.

Carpathia sliced through the water, he hoped the *Titanic* would stay afloat until his ship arrived.

The End

In the deepest parts of the *Titanic*, the situation was growing desperate. Water continued to pour in, and more watertight compartments were filling up. Despite their name, the watertight bulkheads between compartments were not truly watertight: they did not reach all the way to the top deck of the ship. As the *Titanic*'s bow settled lower into the ocean, water from one compartment spilled over into the next one, like water in a tilted ice cube tray. The bow of the *Titanic* was already awash, and every passing minute dragged it farther down.

By now, the passengers were beginning to realize the seriousness of their situation. Many tearful goodbyes were said as wives were placed in the lifeboats at the insistence of their husbands. "It's all right, little girl," Daniel Marvin comforted his wife of three months. "You go and I'll stay a while."[17] Not all of the men showed such courage, however, and soon the deck officers found it increasingly difficult to fill the lifeboats in an orderly manner. Senior officers resorted to brandishing pistols to keep an unruly mob of men from boarding the boats, and some reports describe officers shooting defiant passengers.

Over the next hour and twenty minutes, *Titanic* crewmen managed to launch eighteen of the twenty lifeboats (the last two floated off the deck as the ship foundered). None of the boats was filled to capacity. As one lifeboat was about to begin its descent, Ismay climbed aboard, an act of self-preservation that would haunt him for the rest of his life. At 2:05 a.m. the last lifeboat, carrying around twenty occupants, settled into the sea and headed away from the sinking ship. Left aboard the *Titanic* were

Passengers aboard lifeboats watch in horror as the once-magnificent *Titanic* slides into the ocean depths. Hundreds of people still on the ship had no chance for survival.

more than fifteen hundred passengers and crew with no means of escape.

With the *Titanic's* angle growing steeper by the minute, the orchestra could no longer play on the tilting deck. The musicians wished each other well and parted company. Smith relieved Phillips and Bride of their wireless duties and informed the crew, "It's every man for himself."[18] The captain then headed for the bridge to await his fate. In the first-class smoking room, a dazed Andrews stood by the fireplace. "Aren't you going to have a try for it, Mr. Andrews?"[19] a steward asked. The *Titanic's* designer simply stood there without saying a word.

Did You Know?

Of the approximately 900 *Titanic* crew members, only 214 survived.

Crowds of desperate passengers began scrambling toward the stern, which was rising as the bow settled deeper in the water. Many jumped overboard, hoping to be picked up by a lifeboat. Suddenly, the forward funnel broke free and crashed into the water on top of passengers swimming for their lives. The *Titanic's* lights flickered and went dark. Then, in one terrifying moment, the hull of the *Titanic* could no longer take the strain and ruptured in two between the third and fourth funnels. Loud, groaning noises emanated from the depths of the slanting *Titanic* as boilers, engines, and bulkheads gave way. The forward part slipped under the surface and began its plunge to the bottom; the stern, free from the rest of the ship, settled back into the water. A moment of hope that it might remain afloat was dashed when it began to rise vertically, its three propellers emerging from the sea. Then, like the bow before it, the stern plummeted into the waves, carrying hundreds of screaming passengers with it.

At 2:20 a.m. on April 15, 1912, the *Titanic* passed into history. The broken body of the largest moving object built by human hands settled into the muddy bottom of the North Atlantic.

CHAPTER THREE

Aftermath

With the *Titanic* and her blazing lights gone, the scene in the North Atlantic was one of almost total darkness, save for the faint illumination of the stars above. Cries of help from hundreds of passengers floating in the icy water echoed across the ocean's still surface. Lifeboats carrying the surviving passengers and crew bobbed in the water some distance from the spot where the *Titanic* went down. They had rowed away from the vessel to avoid being pulled under by the suction of the sinking ship. Now, a dilemma presented itself: should the lifeboats return to pick up more survivors?

In several of the boats, some passengers wanted to go back for survivors, but they were outvoted by the rest, who feared that so many people trying to get into the lifeboat would swamp it. In Lifeboat 8, Seaman Thomas Jones and a few others suggested heading back but were overruled. "Ladies, if any of us are saved," Jones declared, "remember I wanted to go back. I would rather drown with them than leave them."[20]

Desertion and Rescue

Quartermaster Hichens was in charge of Lifeboat 6. Among the twenty-five people on board were lookout Fleet, first-class passenger Arthur Peuchen, and an American millionaire named Margaret Brown. Peuchen, a military officer with some boating experience, helped Fleet with rowing while Hichens handled the tiller that moved the rudder. Almost immediately, tensions arose. Afraid that Peuchen might challenge his command, Hichens berated the man and made it quite clear that he, not Peuchen, was in charge. Such bullying did not impress Brown, however, who rallied the women in the boat in an effort to get Hichens to row back and pick up survivors. Hichens callously refused, stating, "There's no use going back, 'cause there's only a lot of stiffs there."[21] He then ordered Peuchen and Fleet to stop rowing and let the lifeboat drift. This was too much for Brown, who knew that some of those left behind were the husbands of the women in the boat. She shoved Hichens aside and grabbed the tiller, urging the women to start rowing to keep warm. When Hichens challenged her, the gutsy Brown reportedly threatened to throw him overboard.

Things were different in Lifeboat 14, commanded by Fifth Officer Harold Lowe. About 150 yards (137 m) from the location of

Seven-year-old Eva Hart, pictured here with her parents in 1912, later recalled the "deathly, terrible silence" after the ship and many of its passengers and crew—her father among them—had disappeared beneath the waves.

the sinking, it encountered Lifeboats 4, 10, 12, and Collapsible D; Lowe lashed the boats together for safety. He then decided to return for survivors and transferred his passengers to the other boats. But Lowe chose to delay his boat's return to reduce the possibility of being capsized by too many survivors. When the lifeboat reached the sinking area, Lowe discovered that his precautions were unnecessary, as most of the people he encountered were already dead. Lifeboat 14 managed to retrieve four men, one of whom soon died. Sometime later, the boat encountered Collapsible A, barely afloat with thirteen passengers aboard. Lowe managed to bring all thirteen into his lifeboat.

With the frigid water taking its toll, it became difficult to locate more survivors. Most of those floating in the water did not actually drown; rather they succumbed to hypothermia, which caused death in fifteen to thirty minutes of exposure to the 28°F (-2°C) ocean. Finally, Lowe called off his search. Survivor Eva Hart, who was seven years old at the time of the *Titanic*'s sinking, remembers the scene. "It seemed as if once everybody had gone, drowned, finished, the whole world was standing still. There was nothing, just this deathly, terrible silence in the dark night with the stars overhead."[22]

The *Carpathia* to the Rescue

On board the *Carpathia*, Rostron prepared his ship to receive survivors of the *Titanic*. The deck crew swung the ship's lifeboats out on their davits (launching cranes) and rigged rope ladders and bosun's chairs (wooden seats suspended by ropes) along the sides of the ship. Stewards gathered as many blankets as they could find, and the galley crew prepared gallons of tea, coffee, and soup. The *Carpathia*'s doctors turned its three dining rooms into makeshift hospital wards and equipped them with emergency medical supplies. The commotion of the preparations woke many of the *Carpathia's* passengers, who helped by donating warm clothing and offering to share their cabins with survivors.

On the bridge, Rostron could do little more than wait and hope as his ship steamed toward the *Titanic's* last reported position. The *Carpathia's* engines were now driving the ship past the maximum speed it was designed to run. At about 2:45 a.m., Second Officer James Bissett saw a dark shape perhaps a mile (1.6 km) ahead — an iceberg. The *Carpathia* was entering the ice field where the *Titanic* had met its end, and Rostron posted extra lookouts at the bow of the ship.

Knowing he was closing in on the *Titanic's* position, Rostron ordered rockets fired at fifteen-minute intervals to alert any survivors that help was on the way. At 3:30 a.m. the *Carpathia* arrived at the last coordinates transmitted by wireless operator Phillips, only to find no *Titanic*, no lifeboats, nothing but open ocean. The *Titanic's* bridge officers had made an error in calculating the coordinates of the ship when it had hit the iceberg, causing Phillips to transmit the wrong location. As Rostron peered out into the night, he saw a small green light shining on the horizon. Believing it indicated that the *Titanic* might still be afloat, the captain headed the *Carpathia* toward the light.

Did You Know?
While many survivors had time to dress warmly, others climbed into the lifeboats wearing only flimsy nightclothes.

Picking Up Survivors

In Lifeboat 2, Fourth Officer Joseph Boxhall was holding a green flare as high over his head as he could, praying that someone, anyone, would see it. He hoped that the crews of other boats would spot the light and row toward it. What he soon saw, however, was not another lifeboat but a white rocket zooming into the night sky, a signal that a rescue ship was approaching. Boxhall waved the flare in a frantic effort to catch the ship's attention.

The Mystery Ship

The ship that lay motionless in the North Atlantic just a few miles from the sinking *Titanic* is usually identified as the *Californian*. But some say there was another ship floating between the *Californian* and the *Titanic*, a ship that had a reason for remaining unidentified.

In 1939 a sailor named Hendrik Naess wrote that he had been on the Norwegian ship *Samson*, which he said was in the area of the sinking *Titanic* on April 14, 1912. The *Samson* was a 147-foot-long (45 m) steamship, a seal-hunting vessel secretly conducting an illegal search for its prey. Naess wrote that the *Samson*'s captain saw the *Titanic*'s distress rockets and, fearing discovery if the signals attracted more ships, ordered his vessel to quickly leave the scene.

Naess's story has never been confirmed. If it were true, it could mean that the ship seen from the beleaguered *Titanic* was the *Samson*, not the *Californian*. This would absolve Captain Lord of blame for not rushing the *Californian* to the *Titanic*'s rescue, as it would have been farther away. Lord also may have assumed the *Titanic* was communicating with the *Samson*.

The *Samson* story has spawned two opposing groups. The first wholeheartedly believes the story and holds Captain Lord blameless. The other contends that tax records indicate the *Samson* was docked in Norway at the time. As with many aspects of the *Titanic* story, the mystery ship may forever remain a mystery.

He was relieved to see that the rescue ship was slowly making its way toward his lifeboat. At 4:00 a.m., the *Carpathia* stopped dead in the water, and Boxhall ordered his boat rowed to its side. The eighteen survivors aboard Lifeboat 2 were the first to be rescued by the *Carpathia*. When Boxhall boarded the *Carpathia*, he went to the bridge where Rostron was waiting. The captain asked, "The *Titanic* has gone down?" Boxhall replied, "Yes, she went down at about 2:30." The captain responded, "Were many people on board when she sank?" Boxhall answered, "Hundreds and hundreds! Perhaps a thousand! Perhaps more!"[23]

With his duty done and his body wracked by cold and grief, Boxhall was taken to one of the *Carpathia*'s makeshift infirmaries to warm up.

Dawn broke over the North Atlantic to reveal a remarkable scene. Dozens of icebergs of all sizes and shapes floated in the

Titanic *survivors are comforted on the deck of the* Carpathia, *as seen in this hand-colored glass slide from 1912. After a brief memorial service, the ship's captain set a course for New York City.*

water north of the *Carpathia*'s location. Alongside the rescue ship, *Titanic* lifeboats discharged their passengers, who climbed to the deck and were helped aboard by the *Carpathia*'s crew. They were then escorted below, where the *Carpathia*'s public rooms had been turned into dormitories.

By 8:30 a.m., all of the *Titanic*'s survivors were aboard the *Carpathia*. Rostron ordered a search for any other survivors. They found none. They saw only one man floating in the water and he was already dead. Then, the *Titanic*'s empty lifeboats were hoisted aboard. The captain held a brief memorial service for those who had been lost, and then he set the *Carpathia* on a course for New York City. Many of the *Titanic*'s women lined the *Carpathia*'s rails for one last sorrowful look at the scene of the tragedy that took their fathers, husbands, and sons from them.

A Missed Opportunity

By the time the *Carpathia* began steaming to New York, other ships had converged on the site of the sinking. The vessels *Virginian*, *Frankfurt*, and *Olympic,* as well as other ships, had all responded to the *Titanic*'s distress messages, but they had been too far away. The one ship that had been near enough to be of any real help to the *Titanic*'s survivors still floated motionless in the water only a few miles in the distance.

At about 4:30 a.m., more than two hours after the *Titanic* had sunk, Lord woke up and made his way to the *Californian*'s bridge. Chief Officer George Stewart asked whether he was going to investigate the ship that had been firing rockets. After looking at the vessel in the distance through binoculars—assuming it was that same ship—Lord replied that it seemed to be all right. The captain was, in fact, observing the *Carpathia*. Stewart was still concerned, so he ran to the wireless room and asked Evans to make a call for any ship that might have information. Soon the terrible truth came back over the airwaves that the *Titanic* was gone. Lord gave the order to take his ship to the coordinates.

At 8:30 a.m., the *Californian* arrived at the spot where the *Carpathia* was picking up the last *Titanic* survivors. All the passengers from the last lifeboat, number 12, had come aboard, followed by Lightoller, the lifeboat's commander and the last survivor to be rescued. Rostron signaled Lord to look for any more survivors in the water, but his task turned out to be futile. Aside from numerous pieces of wreckage, Lord found no survivors and no more bodies floating in the Atlantic. After his search was complete, Lord set a course for the *Californian* to continue on to Boston, its original destination.

Sailing to New York

The clear and bright morning of April 15 seemed somehow incongruous when viewed against the background of the tragedy that had just unfolded. By now, all the passengers of the *Carpathia* were awake, finding 706 *Titanic* survivors now among them on

Did You Know?
At two months of age, Milvinia Dean was the youngest passenger (and survivor) on the *Titanic*. She died in 2009 at the age of ninety-seven.

An Accusation of Bribery

Among the first-class passengers on the *Titanic* were Sir Cosmo Duff Gordon and his wife, Lady Lucy, a wealthy couple from England. On the night of the sinking they got into Lifeboat 1 which, despite its capacity of forty people, carried only twelve, most of whom were crewmen.

As the small boat gained distance from the sinking ship, Sir Cosmo overheard one of the crewmen complaining about his situation. "We have lost our kit," the crewman said, referring to his tools, "and the company won't give us any more." Responding to the sailor's complaint, Sir Cosmo promised to give each man enough money to replace his lost property. After reaching the *Carpathia,* he made good on his promise, but a rumor began circulating about a possible ulterior motive for Sir Cosmo's generosity.

Word spread that the money was not a gift but rather a bribe to the crewmen, either for letting the Duff Gordons onto the lifeboat or to prevent the crew from rowing the boat back to the *Titanic* to pick up survivors, possibly to be swamped by too many people hoping for rescue. Because of this, Lifeboat 1 came to be sarcastically called the "money boat." Sir Cosmo was accused of placing his own safety above helping those whose lives were in peril.

An official investigation cleared Sir Cosmo of any wrongdoing. But he lived out his life under the shadow of a bribery that never occurred.

Quoted in Daniel Allen Butler, *"Unsinkable": The Full Story of RMS* Titanic. Mechanicsburg, PA: Stackpole, 1998, p. 144.

---

board their ship. After learning of the *Titanic*'s sinking, the *Carpathia*'s passengers went out of their way to aid the survivors, donating extra clothing, offering a comforting shoulder, and helping the crew distribute blankets and hot food.

The survivors, still stunned by the sinking and loss of loved ones, found spaces on the deck wherever they could to rest and try to adjust to lives that had been forever changed. Rostron held a service of remembrance for the dead and gratitude for the living. Doctors continued to treat the injured, and a comprehensive listing of the survivors was made in order to inform relatives back home who had survived and who had perished. One survivor was particularly affected by the tragedy. From the moment J. Bruce Ismay came aboard the *Carpathia*, he kept to himself, so distraught by the loss of his ship that he was given a sedative to calm him. Despite his emotional condition, Ismay had to perform the difficult duty of officially informing his company of the loss of the *Titanic*. He wrote the following message to be sent to White Star Line's New York headquarters: "Deeply regret advise you Titanic sank this morning fifteenth after collision iceberg resulting serious loss life. Further particulars later."[24] For some reason, the message was not transmitted until April 17.

The ship's surgeon, Dr. Frank McGhee, gave Ismay exclusive use of his cabin during the trip to New York. Ismay seldom left the cabin, ate little, and, aside from a few visitors, remained isolated from the rest of the people on the *Carpathia*. It was the beginning of a self-imposed distancing from the *Titanic* disaster that would mark the remainder of his life.

A Grim Mission

With the *Titanic* survivors bound for the safety of dry land, one more task fell to a small ship named the CS *Mackay-Bennett*. The vessel's regular job was to maintain and repair underwater communication cables, but it had also performed many maritime rescues. The ship was contracted by the White Star Line to recover the bodies of any *Titanic* victims still afloat in the North Atlantic. On April 17, the *Mackay-Bennett* set sail from Halifax, Nova Scotia, laden with one hundred coffins, embalming supplies, and ice to preserve bodies. When it reached the site of the *Titanic*'s sinking on April 20, crewmen in small boats began retrieving bodies that remained on the surface, buoyed by their life jackets.

Over seven days of arduous work, 306 bodies were recovered by the *Mackay-Bennett*. The crew embalmed 209 of the bodies and brought them to Halifax to be returned to their families or interred in local cemeteries. Another 119 unidentified bodies were buried at sea due to a lack of space on the *Mackay-Bennett*. Nine bodies were retrieved by other ships, bringing the total recovered to 337. The remainder of the *Titanic*'s 1,517 victims went down with the ship or were carried out to sea by wind and waves, lost forever in the cold Atlantic.

CHAPTER FOUR

The Search for the Truth

While the *Carpathia* was heading west toward New York City, newspapers were receiving the first hints that something terrible had happened to the *Titanic*. At around 1:20 a.m. on April 15, Carr Van Anda, the managing editor of the *New York Times*, received a copy of an Associated Press bulletin transmitted from Cape Race: "At 10:25 o'clock tonight [12:15 on the *Titanic*] the White Star Line steamship *Titanic* called 'CQD' to the Marconi station here, and reported having struck an iceberg. The steamer said that immediate assistance was required."[25]

Numerous ships had also received communications from the *Titanic*, messages that were unsettling but short on details. The *Virginian*, located almost 180 miles (290 km) from the sinking ship, reported receiving a "blurred" message at 12:27 a.m. from the *Titanic* that abruptly ended, indicating the possibility of a catastrophic event. With the limited information he had, Van Anda scooped the other newspapers in New York—and in the rest of the country—with the morning edition of the *Times* displaying a shocking four-line headline: "New Liner *Titanic* Hits Iceberg; Sinking by the Bow at Midnight; Women Put Off in Lifeboats; Last Wireless at 12:27 a.m. Blurred."[26]

In another part of New York City, Phillip A.S. Franklin was awakened by the ringing of his telephone. When Franklin, the head of White Star's New York office, answered, a reporter told him that there were reports that the *Titanic* was sinking. Now wide awake, Franklin tried to get details from news organizations, but few hard facts were available. He dressed and hurried to the White Star office, where he and other company officials tried to determine what had happened and how the line should respond. Around 8:00 a.m. news reporters were demanding confirmation of the reports of the *Titanic*'s sinking. Franklin was still skeptical that such a disaster could befall White Star's newest ship, and he made that clear to the press. "We place absolute confidence in the *Titanic*," he informed the reporters. "We believe that the boat is unsinkable."[27]

Did You Know?
A fierce storm battered the *Carpathia* as it made its way to New York with hundreds of *Titanic* survivors onboard.

Franklin's optimism was echoed by newspapers that printed erroneous headlines based on the limited information available. New York's *Evening Sun* announced, "All Saved from *Titanic* After Collision."[28] Another paper reported that the *Titanic*, although damaged, was being towed to Halifax by the *Virginian*. Soon, however, details of what really happened to the *Titanic* were beginning to appear.

The headline on the *New York American*'s April 17 edition told the true fate of the *Titanic* in its headline: "No Hope Left; 1,535 Dead."[29] Crowds began gathering in the street outside the *American*'s headquarters where, on a large chalkboard on the building's second-floor facade, newspaper employees wrote the latest information about the *Titanic* and its survivors. The names of some of the rich and famous survivors were inscribed there: Lady Lucy Duff Gordon, the wife of Scottish landowner Cosmo Duff Gordon; philanthropist Noël, Countess of Rothes; and Madeleine Astor, the young wife of American millionaire John Jacob Astor. As more names were transmitted from the *Carpathia* via wireless to New York, relatives and friends waited anxiously for news of their loved ones.

Word of the Titanic *disaster spreads quickly once newspapers in London (pictured) and elsewhere begin reporting the story. At least one newspaper used a chalkboard outside its office to list the names of survivors as they became known.*

TITANIC DISASTER GREAT LOSS OF LIFE
EVENING NEWS

The *Carpathia's* Return

On the evening of Thursday, April 18, a crowd of nearly thirty thousand gathered at Cunard's Pier 54 in New York to await the arrival of the *Carpathia* with the *Titanic* survivors. Slowly steaming up the Hudson River toward her berth, the *Carpathia* was surrounded by small boats carrying newspaper reporters intent on gathering the latest scoop from the ship's crew. Some reporters held up signs on which questions had been written, and others shouted queries through megaphones. Photographers illuminated the night with their flashes, taking pictures that would appear in the following day's editions.

By 9:30 p.m. the *Carpathia* had docked, and the survivors began leaving the ship that had saved their lives. For some, the reunions with relatives were filled with hugs and smiles; for others, tears were shed for those who would never come home. As the survivors left the *Carpathia*, Franklin boarded the ship and headed to Dr. McGhee's cabin, where he gave Ismay a new suit of clothes and began working with him on a statement to be released to the public about the disaster. Soon a knock on the door signaled the arrival of Senator William Alden Smith, who demanded to speak to Ismay. Despite Franklin's objection that Ismay was too sick to speak to the senator, Smith entered the cabin. As head of a Senate subcommittee charged with investigating the sinking of the *Titanic*, Smith informed Ismay that he was to be a witness at an official inquiry that would begin the next day. Along with questioning survivors, crew, and other people connected with the *Titanic*, Smith hoped that Ismay could answer the tough questions about why his "unsinkable" ship was now on the bottom of the Atlantic Ocean.

The Senate Investigation

The official US Senate inquiry into the *Titanic* disaster was convened at 10:30 a.m. on Friday, April 19, in New York's fashionable Waldorf Astoria hotel. A large conference table had been placed in the center of the hotel's East Room, and rows of chairs were set up for spectators. Shortly after the doors opened, reporters, survivors, and others filled the room. Seated on one side of the table were Smith, Senator Francis G. Newlands, and George Uhler, a ship inspector and Smith's adviser. Across the table sat Ismay, Franklin, and Lightoller. Also present were two bodyguards as protection for Ismay, who had been vilified in the newspapers for saving himself while there were still women and children aboard the *Titanic*.

Ismay was called to give testimony first. Still suffering the effects of the disaster, he was nervous but composed enough to answer Smith's questions. He related the *Titanic*'s voyage and his recollections of the night the ship sank. The subcommittee wanted to know whether the *Titanic* was trying to break a speed record, putting it in danger when it entered iceberg-filled waters. When asked about the *Titanic* steaming to beat the sailing time to New York of the *Olympic*, its sister ship, Ismay replied, "There was nothing to be gained by arriving at New York any earlier."[30] This

After the *Titanic* sank, US Navy ships were tasked with patrolling the area of the sinking to observe and report icebergs that posed a danger to shipping. Soon these vessels were needed for other duties, however, and in 1913 the International Ice Patrol (IIP) was established.

Founded as a direct result of the *Titanic*'s iceberg encounter in the North Atlantic, the IIP is operated today by the US Coast Guard with funding from thirteen nations. During the peak iceberg season—from February 1 through July 31—the IIP patrols the North Atlantic off Newfoundland, where commercial shipping is the heaviest. Primarily using Coast Guard aircraft, the IIP collects iceberg data with special sensors, radar, and visual observation. Data are fed into computers at the IIP operations center in New London, Connecticut, where predicted iceberg locations are calculated and published daily. At one point in its history, the IIP conducted experiments to see whether icebergs could be destroyed with explosives. The effort met with little success and was soon abandoned.

The IIP has been active every year since 1913, except during World Wars I and II. And its safety record is impeccable: no ship that has followed IIP warnings has ever collided with an iceberg. The IIP is an organization that continues to save lives, inspired by the tragic loss of more than fifteen hundred lives more than a century ago.

statement would later be contradicted by a passenger claiming to have overheard Ismay telling Captain Smith that the *Titanic* would beat the *Olympic* to New York by a full day.

During the course of the investigation, eighty-two witnesses gave testimony in person or by affidavit. Among the most significant witnesses were Captain Rostron, who described the rescue of the *Titanic*'s survivors; Lowe, who commanded Lifeboat 14 and its search for survivors; and Lightoller, who was questioned about his role in loading the *Titanic*'s port-side lifeboats and why so many left less than half full. Since wireless played such an important role in the disaster, testimony was given by the *Titanic*'s operator, Bride; by the *Carpathia*'s operator, Harold Cottam; and by the inventor of wireless radio, Guglielmo Marconi.

The Senate inquiry ended on May 25, 1912. But the investigation was not over. British authorities would also have their turn at searching for the truth.

The British Board of Trade Inquiry

Upon learning the news of the *Titanic*'s sinking, the British Board of Trade commissioned an inquiry into the disaster and created the position of Wreck Commissioner to lead the investigation. A prominent British jurist and politician, Judge John Charles Bigham, Lord Mersey of Toxteth, was chosen for the post. Speculation immediately arose among the British public and press that the inquiry would be less than objective since the Board of Trade was responsible for the rules that determined the number of lifeboats British ocean liners were required to carry. It would take nearly two months of testimony to determine whether this would prove true.

Titanic *survivor and managing director of the White Star Line, J. Bruce Ismay, testifies at a US Senate inquiry. Ismay was asked whether the ship was trying to break a speed record. If true, this could have heightened the danger in the iceberg-infested waters.*

Lord Mersey called the inquiry to order on May 2 at the Scottish Drill Hall in London. A cavernous room with a high, vaulted ceiling, the hall featured a platform upon which sat Mersey, along with a group of naval experts who served as his advisers. To one side was a 20-foot (6 m) model of the *Titanic* and a large map of the North Atlantic where the ship had sunk. Over the course of thirty-six days, testimony was heard from many of the same witnesses who had testified in the American inquiry: Ismay, Rostron, Bride, Cottam, Lightoller, and numerous *Titanic* crew members.

Like the Senate inquiry, a major concern of the Board of Trade was determining whether Captain Smith was negligent in steaming at nearly full speed when the ship hit the iceberg. When Ismay was asked whether the *Titanic* was going too fast so close to the ice field, he replied, "Assuming the weather was perfectly fine, I should say the Captain was perfectly justified in going full speed."[31] Ismay also said that he had never spoken to Captain Smith about the *Titanic*'s speed.

Another controversial aspect of the *Titanic* tragedy was the number of lifeboats on board. Harland and Wolff's Alexander Carlisle, who originally thought the *Titanic* should have had more lifeboats, was asked why the ship did not increase its complement of boats. Carlisle explained that the ship had davits that could hold more lifeboats than were required by the Board of Trade, but he had no authority to compel White Star to add more boats beyond the board's minimum requirements.

The Board of Trade also investigated the inaction of the *Californian* on the night of the disaster. Under rigorous interrogation, Captain Lord stated that he felt justified remaining in his cabin while a ship in the distance was firing rockets. "If it had been a distress signal, the Officer on watch would have told me. . . . We sometimes get these company's signals which resemble rockets;

After the US Senate and British Board of Trade inquiries had ended, the participants in the *Titanic* tragedy had to find a way to resume their daily lives. For at least two survivors, the task was not an easy one.

J. Bruce Ismay returned to England a broken man. His presence in a lifeboat and subsequent rescue had earned him the nickname J. *Brute* Ismay in the American press. Once home, he refused to talk about the *Titanic*, and it was not allowed even to be mentioned in his presence. He resigned his chairmanship of the White Star Line and retreated into a life of routine and isolation. He played golf and fished, visited Ireland in the summer, and attended concerts in London by himself. He died of a stroke in 1937, never having completely overcome his reputation as a coward.

Quartermaster Robert Hichens was condemned by the British inquiry for his abusive actions aboard Lifeboat 6. He continued working in the maritime industry on various small ships, but his later life was overshadowed by alcohol, assault, prison, and joblessness. Hichens died a broken man in 1940.

In 2010 Louise Patten, the granddaughter of Charles Lightoller, revealed that her grandfather had blamed Hichens for the *Titanic*'s destruction. She says that Lightoller told her that Hichens had misinterpreted First Officer Murdoch's steering command when the iceberg was sighted and had turned the ship's wheel the wrong way.

they do not shoot as high and they do not explode." When asked about the identity of the ship firing the rockets, Lord replied, "I am positive it was not the 'Titanic.'"[32]

The Recommendations of the Inquiries

Both the Senate and Board of Trade inquiries resulted in several recommendations intended to prevent a disaster like the sinking of the *Titanic* from happening again. These included having enough lifeboats for everyone on board, making sure that crews were trained in lowering and operating the boats, and stipulating that lifeboat drills should be a regular part of each voyage. It was recommended that watertight bulkheads be extended to a ship's highest deck to avoid spillage from one compartment to the next. The Senate inquiry recommended that ships carrying more than one hundred passengers be equipped with two searchlights, and that the wireless system should be manned twenty-four hours a day.

The British inquiry proposed that lookouts be given regular vision examinations and that ships entering ice fields should reduce speed or alter course to minimize collision danger. The inquiry was silent on the topic of having a sufficient number of lifeboats on all passenger liners. Since the board's own regulations were obviously inadequate, the omission of such a discussion led to talk of a whitewash—meaning the board was deliberately avoiding the subject that so obviously put it in a bad light.

Did You Know?

Claims against the White Star Line for property lost during the sinking amounted to about $17 million; only $663,000 was eventually paid.

Both inquiries condemned the actions of Captain Lord of the *Californian* for not responding to the *Titanic*'s distress signals. Lord Mersey declared that the *Californian* could have safely gone to the *Titanic*'s assistance. "Had she done so," Mersey concluded, "she might have saved many if not all of the lives that were lost."[33]

Because of these and other recommended changes, ocean travel was ultimately made safer. Still, the inquiries left many unanswered questions, such as why the *Titanic* sank with such devastating swiftness. It would take an international team of scientists and engineers using sophisticated underwater technology to learn the answer—eighty-four years after the disaster.

CHAPTER FIVE

Discovering the *Titanic*

For more than seven decades the *Titanic* lay on the bottom of the North Atlantic. In the months after the sinking, several proposals were made to find the wreck, but the technology of the day was inadequate for the task. Technology had advanced by the 1980s, but the incorrect coordinates recorded by the *Titanic*'s officers made finding the ship a challenge. The *Titanic* was large but the ocean is infinitely larger.

The discovery of the *Titanic*'s resting place on the ocean floor began with two US Navy nuclear submarines lost during the Cold War. In 1963 the first vessel, the USS *Thresher*, sank during diving tests in the North Atlantic. Five years later the USS *Scorpion* disappeared on a mission to monitor Soviet naval activity in the Atlantic. The entire crews of both submarines were lost. By the 1980s naval officials had become concerned about the nuclear reactors that had powered the *Thresher* and the *Scorpion*. If the reactors were leaking radiation after being corroded by saltwater for decades, it could cause an environmental catastrophe. They began planning a mission to assess the state of the submarines' power plants. Around the same time, a man with the expertise and equipment to lead such a mission was about to approach the US Navy to discuss a different project.

Robert Ballard was a US Navy Reserve officer with a doctoral degree in marine geology and geophysics and a lifelong interest in ships and the sea. In 1967 Ballard was appointed liaison officer to the Woods Hole Oceanographic Institution (WHOI), a nonprofit ocean research facility located on Cape Cod in Massachusetts. Ballard conducted numerous scientific expeditions from WHOI using a three-man mini-submarine called *Alvin*, making him one of the world's most experienced deep-sea oceanographers. But along with his scientific achievements, Ballard had another goal: he wanted to find the *Titanic*.

A Top Secret Mission

Ballard had designed and built *Argo*, an underwater photographic sled fitted with high-tech video cameras. After years of developing and perfecting *Argo,* in 1983 Ballard approached Admiral Ronald Thunman to request navy funding for an expedition to find the *Titanic*. Thunman, however, had a different mission in mind. "I wanted him to go and take a look at where *Thresher* was and where *Scorpion* was,"[34] he later revealed. Thunman offered navy funding for a survey of the sunken submarines, keeping the mission top secret to avoid Soviet spying. After Ballard completed that mission, he could use any time left to look for the *Titanic*. Although Thunman did not believe that Ballard would find the *Titanic*, he knew the search for the legendary wreck would provide a good cover story for the covert submarine mission.

Did You Know?
During Ballard's third dive to the *Titanic*, a small remote-controlled robot called *Jason Junior* entered the wreck and traveled down the Grand Staircase.

Summer is the best time to conduct deep ocean research, when wind and waves are most likely to cooperate. In July 1984, Ballard began his survey of the *Thresher*, which lay 8,400 feet (2,560 m) below the surface of the Atlantic. Using *Argo*, Ballard recorded images of the *Thresher* and a large debris field of objects spilled from the broken submarine (including its nuclear reactor). Tests of the reactor revealed no leakage of radioactive material. Having com-

Robert Ballard gives a thumbs-up sign on his return from the site of the sunken Titanic in 1986. Beside him is Jason Junior, the small remote-controlled robot used to explore the wreckage in the North Atlantic.

pleted the first part of his mission for the US Navy, Ballard began planning his *Titanic* mission, which would take place the next year.

The search for the *Titanic* would be a two-phase expedition. Ballard and his team from WHOI would work with scientists from France's national oceanographic institution, known by the acronym IFREMER. According to the plan, the French would carry out the first phase, locating the wreck using a side-scan sonar vehicle known as SAR. Towed underwater by a ship, the SAR vehicle uses pulses of sound to form images of underwater objects. In phase two, Ballard and his team would use *Argo* to document the wreck with its high-resolution video cameras.

The IFREMER team's research vessel, *Le Suroit*, left France on June 24, 1985, and reached the area of the *Titanic*'s sinking on July 5. The French team deployed the SAR vehicle, lowering it to about 600 feet (183 m) above the seabed by a cable attached to *Le Suroit*. The ship began to tow the vehicle across the search

Robert Ballard was not the only person interested in discovering the *Titanic*. Jack Grimm, a wealthy Texas oilman with a fondness for exploring the unknown, had sponsored expeditions to find Noah's ark and the Loch Ness monster. Now "Cadillac" Jack, as he was known, set his sights on a new quest: finding the *Titanic*.

In July 1980 Grimm sent two oceanographers on the ship *H.J.W. Fay* to conduct the search. Ever the promoter, Grimm had come up with a bizarre publicity stunt to guarantee press coverage. He hired a monkey to point out on a map where the *Titanic* could be found. When his oceanographers called the stunt an affront to the serious nature of the search, the monkey was left behind.

Arriving at the location of the *Titanic*'s last distress call, the scientists began scanning the ocean bottom with sonar. The device discovered nothing conclusive, but it did reveal several *Titanic*-sized targets. Grimm hinted to the press that the *Titanic* had been found. Once again, the oceanographers stepped up to retract that bit of misinformation.

A second expedition was mounted in 1981, this time with Grimm along. Using video, another look at the targets found on the first trip confirmed they were merely natural formations. Growing desperate, Grimm claimed another object spotted was one of the *Titanic*'s propellers, but this, too, proved false. After a failed third expedition, Cadillac Jack gave up, leaving the *Titanic* waiting silently to be discovered by Ballard.

area in back-and-forth passes, similar to mowing a lawn. The scientists were searching an area of some 132 square miles (343 sq. km) where calculations indicated the wreck of the *Titanic* might be. In the four weeks allotted to explore the ocean bottom, the IFREMER team covered more than 70 percent of the search area but found no trace of the *Titanic*. It was now time to begin phase two.

Twelve Days

Before he could look for the *Titanic*, Ballard had to complete his navy mission by surveying the wreck of the *Scorpion*, which had sunk some 400 miles (644 km) off the Azores in the eastern Atlantic. Sailing on the WHOI research vessel RV *Knorr*, Ballard had brought along several members of the IFREMER team to help locate the *Titanic*. He had to be careful not to divulge the details of the secret submarine mission to the French scientists. The survey of the *Scorpion*'s debris field revealed that its nuclear reactor, like the *Thresher*'s, was intact and posed no environmental danger. His secret mission now accomplished, Ballard ordered the *Knorr* to head west toward Newfoundland. He had twelve days left to find the *Titanic*.

The *Knorr* arrived at the search area on August 24, 1985. Ballard's team would conduct the search from a control van on the deck of the *Knorr*. A large blue box built from two shipping containers, the van was crammed with video monitors, computers, and joystick controls that a technician would use to remotely "fly" *Argo* through the deep ocean.

Ballard had some new ideas for conducting this phase of the search. Recalling how the debris fields of the *Thresher* and the *Scorpion* were so much larger than the submarines themselves, and thus were easier to find, Ballard decided that he would try to locate the *Titanic*'s debris field, which he could then follow to the wreck. Also, since IFREMER's sonar search had come up empty, Ballard would instead rely on a visual search using *Argo*'s video cameras. On August 25 *Argo* was lowered beneath the surface of the Atlantic to begin its more than 2-mile-deep (3 km) descent to the bottom.

Discovery

For a week, *Argo* scanned the search area without success. In the control van, the video monitors displayed what *Argo*'s cameras were seeing: acres of gray, featureless mud, with no sign of the *Titanic* or its debris field. For the engineers and scientists in the van, fighting boredom was a constant battle. At midnight on Sunday, September 1, a new watch began, and the relief crew settled into their positions while Ballard retired to his cabin to get some sleep.

Shortly before 1:00 a.m., engineer Stu Harris, his eyes glued to a video monitor, quietly said, "There's something." In an instant, boredom evaporated as everyone stared at the monitor. Another voice soon broke the silence: "Wreckage!"[35] The crew cheered as images of objects that were obviously not natural to an ocean environment appeared on the screen. But there was no way to tell whether they came from the *Titanic*. *Argo* continued its search path, and soon the image of a large round object lying in the mud came into view. Someone quickly thumbed through a reference book containing photographs of the *Titanic*, stopping at a picture of a round object identical to the image on the screen: one of the ship's twenty-nine boilers. Ballard's team had discovered the wreck of the doomed liner.

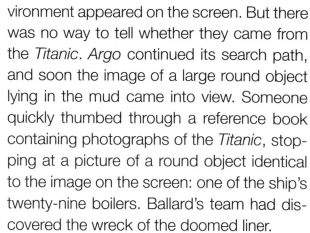

Did You Know?
Although jackets, shoes, and other items of clothing were discovered, all traces of human remains have long since been devoured by sea creatures.

When Ballard was informed of the finding, he pulled his jumpsuit on over his pajamas and raced to the van, where he watched a videotape replay of the moment of discovery. The cheers of the crew soon gave way to an awed silence as *Argo* passed over more wreckage, which Ballard later described:

> On *Argo*'s monitors we watched a procession of bronze portholes, twisted sections of railing, hull plating and small deck equipment stream by on the rolling gray mud of the bottom. Most of us had forgotten how huge a ship *Titanic* had been, that she had been assembled from hundreds and thousands of these individual bits and pieces, now revealed to human eyes in the glare of *Argo*'s floodlights for the first time in seventy-three years.[36]

At 2:20 a.m., the exact time the *Titanic* sank, scientists, technicians, and crew gathered at the stern of the *Knorr* as Ballard raised the flag of the ship's builder, Harland and Wolff. "I really don't have much to say," he remarked, "but I thought we might just observe a few moments of silence." After paying respects to the more than fifteen hundred souls lost in the sinking, Ballard said, "Thank you all. Now let's get back to work."[37]

Completing the Mission

While Ballard's team had discovered the debris field, they still had to find the main wreckage itself. Despite all the high-tech equipment at their disposal, it was a piece of old-fashioned technology that located the *Titanic*'s hull. The *Knorr*'s echo sounder, an instrument that uses sound to measure ocean depth, picked up a large object located directly underneath it. The massive size of the object left no doubt as to its identity. The *Titanic*'s hull had been found.

With only a few days left and a storm approaching, numerous video and photo runs were made of the wreck using *Argo* and an unmanned still-camera sled called ANGUS. Images from *Argo* showed the *Titanic*'s bow resting on the seabed, relatively intact

The frame of a metal deck bench from the *Titanic* can be seen amid other wreckage on the ocean floor. Other items that could be seen in underwater video included one of the ship's boilers, bronze portholes, and twisted sections of railing.

and covered in rusticles—red, orange, and yellow formations of rust that gave the appearance of icicles. The first funnel was missing, and the foremast, with the crow's nest still attached, had fallen backward onto the remains of the bridge. As *Argo* moved along the hull, its images showed that the front section of the *Titanic* ended in a ragged tangle of mangled steel, with the debris field trailing behind it. Photographs from ANGUS later revealed that the stern was lying 1,970 feet (600 m) from the bow. It had spun 180 degrees in its descent and, unlike the bow, had imploded from the force of water pressure, crushing it into an almost unrecognizable mass on the ocean floor.

Did You Know?
A 1987 expedition to the *Titanic* recovered a leather satchel from the wreckage containing coins, bank notes, and jewels.

Although there was much more to be learned on the expedition, Ballard's time was up. As the *Knorr* began its voyage home, a weary Ballard conducted media interviews by radio. When the *Knorr* pulled into the harbor at Woods Hole on September 9, crowds of local well-wishers, news media, and Woods Hole representatives greeted the expedition with cheers, a band, and a cannon salute. In many ways it was reminiscent of the fanfare that attended the launch of the *Titanic*'s hull on May 31, 1911. In the long span of years between these two dates, the *Titanic* was created, destroyed, and then left undisturbed at the bottom of the ocean.

Further Expeditions

Since the discovery of the *Titanic*, numerous expeditions have been made to the wreck site. Ballard returned to the *Titanic* several times, diving to the bottom of the Atlantic in the submersible *Alvin*. Other expeditions included those by a Russian-Canadian-American consortium, IFREMER, the US National Oceanic and Atmospheric Administration, and filmmaker James Cameron for his 1997 blockbuster film *Titanic*. Between 1987 and 2004 more than

The *Titanic* Reborn

More than a century after the *Titanic's* sinking, the allure of sailing on such a magnificent luxury liner has not faded. Someday, passengers may be able to relive the elegance of the *Titanic's* maiden voyage (minus the iceberg) on a new ship named the *Titanic II*.

The brainchild of Australian entrepreneur Clive Palmer, the *Titanic II* was conceived in 2012 as the flagship liner for a new company called the Blue Star Line. Slated to be built in China, the new ship will be identical to the original in length, but it will be several feet wider to increase stability. Other improvements will include a welded, rather than riveted, hull; diesel engines replacing coal-fired steam engines; a new "safety deck" to provide an adequate number of lifeboats; and modern navigation technology. The interior of the *Titanic II* is planned to resemble the original as closely as possible, with luxurious dining saloons, cabins, and promenade decks. The famous first-class Grand Staircase will also be re-created.

While water tank tests of *Titanic II* models were performed, building of the ship faced numerous delays due to financial and legal problems. In September 2018 the Blue Star Line announced that these problems were resolved and construction was ready to begin. "The *Titanic* was the ship of dreams," says Palmer. "Millions have dreamt of sailing on her. . . . *Titanic II* will be the ship where those dreams come true."

Quoted in Blue Star Line, "Palmer Building *Titanic II*," press release, September 27, 2018. http://blue starline.com.au.

---

five thousand artifacts were recovered from the *Titanic's* wreckage. They included passengers' personal belongings—items such as cups, plates, wine bottles, and silverware; pieces of the ship itself, including the crow's nest bell; and chunks of coal. Among these artifacts were several objects that held a clue to the real reason the ship sank.

Because the lower part of the *Titanic's* bow section is buried in the mud of the ocean bottom, a visual inspection of the area where the iceberg hit was impossible. But some of the millions of rivets that held the *Titanic's* hull together were recovered. Metallurgical tests of these rivets revealed that an inferior grade of iron had been used in their manufacture. Scientists concluded that when the *Titanic* struck the iceberg, the pressure on the hull forced the heads of the rivets to pop off, causing hull plates to separate and allowing water to surge into the ship. With this new evidence, the original theory of why the *Titanic* sank—a 300-foot-long (91 m) gash in its hull—was replaced by a much smaller breach of the hull plates, six gaps with a total area estimated at only about 12 square feet (1 sq. m).

The *Titanic*'s Legacy

Ballard has criticized the numerous dives made to the *Titanic* over the years, asserting that careless exploration is accelerating the deterioration of the fragile wreck. For others, the expeditions represent a desecration of the final resting place of more than fifteen hundred people who perished on that frigid night in 1912. *Titanic* survivor Eva Hart was outspoken in her criticism of *Titanic* souvenir hunters. "To bring up those things from a mass sea grave . . . shows a dreadful insensitivity and greed. The grave should be left alone. They're simply going to do it as fortune hunters, vultures, pirates!"[38]

Amid the commotion of his return to Woods Hole in 1985, Ballard reflected on his discovery and its meaning for the legacy of those who had died. To an assembled crowd of media representatives, he offered a moving epitaph for the ship he had sought for so long:

> The *Titanic* lies in 13,000 feet of water on a gently sloping alpine-like countryside overlooking a small canyon below. Its bow faces north and the ship sits upright on the bottom. There is no light at this great depth and little life can be found. It is a quiet and peaceful and fitting place for the remains of this greatest of sea tragedies to rest. May it forever remain that way and may God bless these found souls.[39]

SOURCE NOTES

Introduction: An Ill-Fated Voyage

1. Quoted in Titanic Universe, "*Titanic*: The Unsinkable Ship." www.titanicuniverse.com.
2. Quoted in Walter Lord, *A Night to Remember*. New York: Henry Holt, 1955, p. 50.

Chapter One: The Magnificent *Titanic*

3. Shan F. Bullock, *Thomas Andrews, Shipbuilder*. Dublin: Maunsel, 1912, p. 5.
4. Anton Gill, *Titanic: Building the World's Most Famous Ship*. Guilford, CT: Lyons, 2010, p. 178.
5. Quoted in Peter Chrisp, *Explore* Titanic. Hauppauge, NY: Barron's, 2011, n.p.
6. Quoted in Richard Davenport-Hines, *Voyagers of the* Titanic: *Passengers, Sailors, Shipbuilders, Aristocrats, and the Worlds They Came From*. New York: Morrow, 2012, p. 109.
7. Quoted in Encyclopedia Titanica, "Miss Edith Louise Rosenbaum." www.encyclopedia-titanica.org.

Chapter Two: Disaster Strikes

8. Quoted in Daniel Allen Butler, *"Unsinkable": The Full Story of RMS* Titanic. Mechanicsburg, PA: Stackpole, 1998, p. 63.
9. Quoted in Susan Wels, Titanic: *Legacy of the World's Greatest Ocean Liner*. Alexandria, VA: Time-Life, 1997, p. 84.

10. Quoted in Butler, *"Unsinkable,"* p. 67.
11. Quoted in Brad Matsen, Titanic*'s Last Secrets: The Further Adventures of Shadow Divers John Chatterton and Richie Kohler*. New York: Twelve, p. 163.
12. Quoted in Stephen Cox, *The* Titanic *Story: Hard Choices, Dangerous Decisions.* Chicago: Open Court, 1999, p. 68.
13. Quoted in Megan Garber, "The Technology That Allowed the *Titanic* Survivors to Survive," *Atlantic*, April 13, 2012. www.theatlantic.com.
14. Quoted in Matsen, Titanic*'s Last Secrets,* p. 167.
15. Quoted in Cox, *The* Titanic *Story*, p. 69.
16. Quoted in Butler, *"Unsinkable,"* p. 163.
17. Quoted in Lord, *A Night to Remember*, p. 62.
18. Quoted in Robert D. Ballard, *The Discovery of the* Titanic. Toronto: Madison, 1987, p. 222.
19. Quoted in Greg Ward, *The Rough Guide to the* Titanic. London: Rough Guides, 2012, p. 71.

Chapter 3: Aftermath

20. Quoted in Davenport-Hines, *Voyagers of the* Titanic, p. 253.
21. Quoted in Butler, *"Unsinkable,"* pp. 147–48.
22. Quoted in Encyclopedia Titanica, "Miss Eva Miriam Hart." www.encyclopediatitanica.org.
23. Quoted in Daniel Allen Butler, *The Other Side of the Night: The* Carpathia*, the* Californian*, and the Night the* Titanic *Was Lost.* Philadelphia: Casemate, 2011, p. 105.
24. Quoted in John Maxtone-Graham, Titanic *Tragedy: A New Look at the Lost Liner.* New York: Norton, 2011, p. 166.

Chapter 4: The Search for the Truth

25. Quoted in Wyn Craig Wade, *The* Titanic: *End of a Dream*. New York: Penguin, 1986, p. 30.
26. Quoted in Wade, *The* Titanic, p. 31.
27. Quoted in Ward, *The Rough Guide to the* Titanic, p. 139.

28. Quoted in Daniel Mendelsohn, "Unsinkable: Why We Can't Let Go of the *Titanic*," *New Yorker*, April 16, 2012. www .newyorker.com.

29. *New York American*, April 17, 1912. Heritage Auctions. www .historical.ha.com.

30. Quoted in Titanic Inquiry Project, "United States Senate Inquiry: Day 1." www.titanicinquiry.org.

31. Quoted in Titanic Inquiry Project, "British Wreck Commissioner's Inquiry: Day 16." www.titanicinquiry.org.

32. Quoted in Titanic Inquiry Project, "British Wreck Commissioner's Inquiry: Day 7." www.titanicinquiry.org.

33. Quoted in Titanic Inquiry Project, "British Wreck Commissioner's Inquiry Report: Circumstances in Connection with the SS *Californian*." www.titanicinquiry.org.

Chapter 5: Discovering the *Titanic*

34. Quoted in Edmund H. Mahony, "Lost Submarine *Thresher's* Cold War Legacy Includes Discovery of the *Titanic*," *Hartford (CT) Courant*, April 13, 2013. http://articles.courant.com.

35. Quoted in Ballard, *The Discovery of the* Titanic, p. 81.

36. Robert D. Ballard and Malcolm McConnell, *Explorations: My Quest for Adventure and Discovery Under the Sea*. New York. Hyperion, 1995, p. 267.

37. Ballard and McConnell, *Explorations,* p. 269.

38. Quoted in Robert D. Ballard and Michael S. Sweeney, *Return to* Titanic: *A New Look at the World's Most Famous Lost Ship.* Washington, DC: *National Geographic*, 2004, pp. 73–74.

39. Quoted in Ballard, *The Discovery of the* Titanic, p. 101.

FOR FURTHER RESEARCH

Books

Robert D. Ballard with Rick Archbold, *The Discovery of the* Titanic. New York: Grand Central, 1995.

Richard Davenport-Hines, *Voyagers of the* Titanic: *Passengers, Sailors, Shipbuilders, Aristocrats, and the Worlds They Came From.* New York: Morrow, 2012.

Editors of *Life*, Titanic: *The Tragedy That Shook the World: One Century Later*. Des Moines, IA: Life Books, 2012.

Walter Lord, *A Night to Remember: The Classic Account of the Final Hours of the* Titanic. New York: Holt, 2015.

Tim Maltin and Eloise Aston, *101 Things You Thought You Knew About the* Titanic . . . *but Didn't!* New York: Penguin, 2010.

Internet Sources

Dan Bilefsky, "Coal Fire, Not Just Iceberg, Doomed the Titanic, a Journalist Claims," *New York Times*, January 3, 2017. www.nytimes.com.

Robert Khederian, "Why Gilded Age Ocean Liners Were So Luxurious," Curbed, December 21, 2017. www.curbed.com.

Lady Louise Patten, "Did Murdoch Make a Fatal Steering Error?," The Life and Mystery of First Officer William Murdoch. www.williammurdoch.net.

Jason Ponic, "The SS *Californian:* The Ship That Watched *Titanic* Sink," Owlcation, March 4, 2018. www.owlcation.com.

Oliver Smith, "Titanic: 40 Fascinating Facts About the Ship," *Telegraph* (London), April 11, 2017. www.telegraph.co.uk.

Websites

Biography: *Titanic* Passengers (www.biography.com). This website presents comprehensive biographies of some of the major players in the *Titanic* saga: J. Bruce Ismay, John Jacob Astor IV, "Unsinkable" Molly Brown, and many others. It includes some photographs and videos.

Encyclopedia Titanica (www.encyclopedeiatitanica.org). One of the most comprehensive *Titanic* websites, it includes such features as research articles, *Titanic* deck plans, a message board, passenger and crew lists, and historic photographs. The *Titanic* People Explorer allows visitors to browse a massive database by passenger class, crew names, victims or survivors, and other search criteria.

National Archives: *Titanic* 100 Years, 1912–2012 (www.nationalarchives.gov.uk). This website of the British National Archives contains such *Titanic* features as passenger and crew stories, videos and podcasts, a searchable passenger database, and educational resources.

Titanic Inquiry Project (www.titanicinquiry.org). This website contains the official transcripts of the US Senate and British Board of Trade inquiries. It is searchable by day of inquiry and witness name and includes final reports from both investigations.

Woods Hole Oceanographic Institution (www.whoi.edu). This website has information on the *Titanic* that includes multimedia features, composite photographs of the wreck, and information on the numerous expeditions made to the *Titanic*. Also available is information about the institute's research vessels and underwater remotely operated vehicles.

INDEX

PICTURE CREDITS